Thirteen Movements
to Stretch the Body *and* Make it
More Supple,
AND Guiding and
Harmonising Energy TO Regulate
the Breath

Thirteen Movements
to Stretch the Body *and* Make it
More Supple,
AND Guiding and
Harmonising Energy TO Regulate
the Breath

DAO YIN YANG SHENG GONG

Foundation Sequences 2

PROFESSOR ZHANG GUANGDE
Commentary by Zhu Mian Sheng and André Perret

SINGING
DRAGON

LONDON AND PHILADELPHIA

First published in 2011
by Singing Dragon
an imprint of Jessica Kingsley Publishers
116 Pentonville Road
London N1 9JB, UK
and
400 Market Street, Suite 400
Philadelphia, PA 19106, USA

www. singingdragon.com

Library of Congress Cataloging in Publication Data
Guangde, Zhang.
 [Treize mouvements pour ?tirer et assouplir le corps : Guide et harmoniser l'?nergie pour r?gulariser la respiration. English.]
  Thirteen movements to stretch the body and make it more supple, and guiding and harmonising energy to regulate the breath / Zhang Guangde ; translated by Andre Perret.
    p. cm. -- (Foundation sequences in Dao Yin Yang Sheng Gong ; v. 2)
  ISBN 978-1-84819-071-9 (alk. paper)
 1. Qi gong. I. Perret, Andre. II. Title.
  RA781.8.G83 2011
  613.7'1489--dc23
                         2011017020

British Library Cataloguing in Publication Data
A CIP catalogue record for this book is available from the British Library

ISBN 978 1 84819 071 9

Printed and bound in Great Britain by the MPG Book Group

Contents

Professor Zhang Guangde

Born in Tangshan in the province of Hebei, China, in March 1932, Zhang Guangde, Professor at the Beijing University of Physical Education, is one of the greatest masters of Chinese martial arts and has been granted the title of eighth duan in this field.

Professor Zhang is the honorary president of the *Dao Yin* Centre of the same university and former president of the commission of *Dao Yin* of the Association of Higher Education in China.

At the age of 20 he began the practice of martial arts in his home town, and then continued at the department of martial arts at the Beijing University of Physical Education where he completed his studies in 1959. In 1963 he was one of the first generation of graduate research students in this field. He taught martial arts at the University for 45 years and has become one of its most famous pupils.

He has spent nearly 40 years creating and developing his own system: *Yang Sheng Tai Ji* and *Dao Yin Yang Sheng*. This system is based on the philosophy of the *I Ching*, as well as the principal theories of Traditional Chinese Medicine such as meridians, *Yin* and *Yang*, the five elements, *Qi* and blood. This method has shown remarkable effectiveness in maintaining health, and for the prevention and treatment of chronic diseases. His work unites six aspects: *I Ching*, medicine, martial arts, art, music and beauty. Professor Zhang's teaching is imbued with his exceptional personal qualities and has been received warmly everywhere in China.

Dao Yin Yang Sheng Gong has gained the National Prize for Technical Progress in Physical Education and a great many other awards. It forms part of the Chinese national programme for the improvement of the health of the people.

Professor Zhang has written some 30 books in China and published a score of articles that have gained many awards in the national congresses of martial arts.

In addition to teaching practitioners who come to China to study *Dao Yin* with him, Professor Zhang has lectured frequently in more than 20 countries such as Japan, France, Germany, Australia, Singapore, Great Britain, the United States and others, in order to raise awareness of the Chinese culture of wellbeing. Today, more than four million people in China and throughout the world practise *Dao Yin Yang Sheng Gong*.

In 2005 he created the International Institute of *Dao Yin Yang Sheng Gong* (IIDYYSG) in Biarritz, France.

Preface

Zhu Mian Sheng

O riginally *Dao Yin* was an ancient Taoist technique (Fang Shu) used to experience the connection between mankind and Nature. Later it was practised to obtain longevity. *Dao Yin* was known throughout the 'Spring and Autumn',[1] 'Warring States'[2] and 'Hundred Schools of Thought'[3] periods. Many methods are described in Taoist books such as *Zhuang Zi* and *Huai Nan Zi*. In the chapter *Ke Yi* of the *Zhuang Zi* is a text summarising *Dao Yin* as it was practised at that time:

> To inhale, exhale, long breath, short breath, such is breathing. To reject what the body and the mind have used up (impurities); to receive new air (purity); to stretch the body like the bear, to extend and gently turn the neck and arms like a bird its wings, in order to achieve and fulfil the ideal of longevity. This is the rightful goal: the aim of those who practise *Dao Yin*, who maintain and invigorate their own bodies, of those who, like Master *Peng Zu*, achieved the greatest longevity.

---

1   Spring and Autumn Period: from 722 to 481 BC.
2   Warring States Period: from 475 to 221 BC. It ended with the advent of the first emperor.
3   Hundred Schools of Thought Period: during the Warring States Period, the kings and princes called upon itinerant men of letters to consolidate their authority, hence the expression. Hundred Schools is used to describe this period in which Chinese philosophy reached its peak.

The *Tao Te Jing* of Lao Zi is considered to be the philosophical basis of the technique of *Yang Sheng Shu* (the Taoist method of maintaining longevity).

For example, in Chapter 25 of the *Tao Te Jing* it says, 'The *Tao* is great, Heaven is great, the Earth is great, Man also is great. In the Universe four things are great and Man is one of them. Man follows the law of the Earth, the Earth follows the law of Heaven, Heaven follows the law of the Tao and the Tao follows the law of its own nature.' Man unites with Heaven and Earth, following the natural law of the Tao.

In Chapter 10 of the *Tao Te Jing* it says, 'Support, embrace and unify *Ying* (the physical body) and *Po* (the spirit). Do not separate them. Lead and gather *Qi* (energy), to make it soft like a newborn baby. Purify the mind, eliminate disorders from *Xun Lan* (the mysterious inner vision).' The great principle is to calm the mind, regulate the breathing, thus bringing the entire body and the heart into a soft, calm, and more harmonious state.

In Chapter 42 of the *Tao Te Jing* it says, 'Ten thousand beings carry the *Yin* and embrace the *Yang*. *Zong Qi* (vital energy) circulates and *Yin* and *Yang* are harmonised.' This is the essential theory of *Qi*.

In Chapter 45 it says, 'Purity and calm are the rule, and order everything under Heaven.' Thus purity and calm are perceived as universal principles.

All these texts provide the principal theories of *Dao Yin Yang Sheng Shu*. This is why, during the Han Period, *Dao Yin* was called '*Xian Shu*' (the technique of the wise) by the Taoists: 'The ancient sage practises *Dao Yin*, as the bear stretches its back and the bird turns its neck, stretching and folding his loins and moving all the joints of his body, in order to control ageing.'[4]

Chinese traditional medicine, in ancient times called *Huang Lao Yi Xue* (*Huang*: Taoist school, *Lao*: Lao Zi, *Yi Xue*: medicine), has been used since the creation of *Dao Yin* as a means of understanding

---

4 From *The History of the Three Kingdoms*, 'The History of Hua Tuo', a famous surgeon doctor of the period.

and experiencing the human body and, as *Dao Yin* developed, as a method of prevention and care. In the four chapters of the *Huang Di Nei Jing*, *Dao Yin* is identified along with *Xing Qi* (circulating energy), acupuncture, the pharmacopoeia, *An Qiao* (energetic massage), *Yun Fu* (producing heat on parts of the body), for treating various diseases: rheumatism and muscular weakness due to cold or heat, *Xi Ji* (blocking energy), etc. In the *Jin Gui Yiao Lue* of the Han Period, Zhang Zhongjing stressed the preventive effects of *Dao Yin*: 'When feeling the beginning of heaviness in the four limbs, immediately begin practising *Dao Yin*, *Tu Na* (breathing), acupuncture, *Gao Mo* (massage with ointments). Do not wait for the closing and blockage of the nine openings.' In his book *Bao Pu Zi*, Ge Hong, a master Taoist and celebrated doctor of the Eastern Jin era, summarised the effects of *Dao Yin* thus:

> *Dao Yin* treats the condition 'not yet sick', it releases inharmonious energy. The movements must be practised in order to circulate energy without discomfort in the hundred joints. Without movement, blood remains blocked in the three palaces. *Dao Yin* uses this great rule to maintain health and is a subtle and complex technique for eliminating all diseases.

Dao Yin then developed in two directions: with the Taoists, who developed the practice of manufacturing internal cinnabar, and with doctors and practitioners who used it to maintain health. Gradually the latter created various methods, of which the most well known are: *Wu Qin Xi* (the five animal exercises), *Ba Duan Jin* (eight brocades) and *Yi Jin Jing* (the tendons and muscles reinforcing classic).

Returning to the source, what are the essential keys of ancient *Dao Yin*? What are the essential points of this health-maintaining method, called *Yang Sheng Shu* by the Taoists, which has survived for more than 2000 years and which is based on a dynamic mixture of philosophy, medicine, martial arts, etc.? It is really difficult to answer this question.

Zhang Guangde, Professor of the Beijing University of Physical Education, eighth duan in Chinese martial arts, and creator of *Dao Yin Yang Sheng Gong*, is an authority in this field, with 60 years of high level practice in martial arts, over 40 years of teaching and more than 30 years experience disseminating his method in China and a score of countries. He has created four foundation sequences of *Dao Yin Yang Sheng Gong*. Through these four methods the above question is answered precisely and simply, in practice and theory. Many practitioners of *Dao Yin* – specialists and non-specialists alike – pursue a continued study of these four sequences, finding many subtle nuances in their finesse, simplicity and effectiveness, which make them more than simply a preparation for the broader practice of *Dao Yin*.

I have known Professor Zhang for almost 20 years. Impressed by his character and the quality of his system and his theoretical knowledge, in 1992 I introduced *Dao Yin Yang Sheng Gong* to the University of Paris's Faculty of Medicine in Bobigny. Since 1997, when the diploma of Chinese medicine was created in the same faculty, *Dao Yin* has been part of the syllabus for this diploma. In 2004 Doctor André Perret and I founded the International Institute of *Dao Yin Yang Sheng Gong* (IIDYYSG), under the direction of Professor Zhang, to provide the opportunity for detailed and in-depth study of his method.

Some years ago I told my friends that Professor Zhang and his system are for me extraordinary in three ways – extraordinary man, extraordinary system, extraordinary results. This is still my view today, which is why I have agreed to accept responsibility on behalf of the Institute to translate the sequences chosen and verified by Professor Zhang. In these first two books, we begin with the four foundation sequences.

Editorial Preface

Zhu Mian Sheng, André Perret and Yolande Mano

We have waited for five years before publishing this translation of the foundation sequences. These five years of additional training with Professor Zhang Guangde have enabled us to gain a global understanding of his method, and of his teaching. We have tried to reproduce as far as possible the basis and form of this teaching, through the choice of terms used and the additional notes and appendices. With this aim in mind, we have produced this book according to the following principles:

1. To translate the original work of Professor Zhang Guangde as faithfully as possible in its entirety.

2. To enable a better comprehension of the main text by including supplementary concepts contributed by Professor Zhang Guangde, Zhu Mian Sheng or André Perret in notes or appendices.

3. To assume that the reader already knows, albeit perhaps only a little, some basic theory (*Yin Yang, Wu Xing, Zhang Fu, Jing Luo*: Yin-Yang, the five elements, the organs and entrails, the meridians). Therefore we have included further theoretical information contributed by Professor Zhang Guangde and Zhu Mian Sheng.

4. To retain the Chinese characters for certain important words, in addition to the translation offered, to allow the informed reader to do his own research on these terms.

5. To capture as closely as possible in the translation the movement and feeling described. For example, 'draw in the buttocks' rather than 'tighten the buttocks', because it is possible to tighten the buttocks without causing movement in the pelvis or *Ming Men*. Similarly 'release the lumbar region' rather than 'relax the lumbar region', because the releasing of the lumbar muscles causes their passive stretching, etc.

6. To retain the *Pin Yin* version of the important names current at the time of Professor Zhang's teaching, for example *Dan Tian, Yuan, Gu Dao, Que Qiao*, explaining these words, in notes or appendices, when they first appear in the text.

7. To keep the Chinese *Pin Yin* name for points and meridians. In the text the name is given rather than the number of the acupuncture point, because in the practice of *Dao Yin* it is the zone corresponding to the name that is worked and not strictly the point itself. Second, the name of the point gives more information about its particular characteristics than does just its number. Finally, Professor Zhang Guangde prefers that his pupils make the effort to know the names of the points used, their significance and their function, to develop a deeper understanding of *Dao Yin*. However, in order to help the reader we also give, on its first appearance in the text, the number of the point. Thereafter, the corresponding number will be found in Appendix 4.

8. To clarify the technical description with video footage intended for training and corrections, but not for use in regular practice. This is because *Dao Yin* requires to be practised at the appropriate rhythm while concentrating on oneself and not on an image on a screen.

PART 1

Thirteen Movements to Stretch the Body and Make it More Supple

引體令柔十三式

Yin Ti Ling Rou Shi San Shi

第五勢 di wu shi 躬身 gong shen 弔尾 diao wei 勢 shi	第四勢 di si shi 舒胸 shu xiong 仰體 yang ti 勢 shi	第三勢 di san shi 托天 tuo tian 旋轉 xuan zhuan 勢 shi	第二勢 di er shi 左右 zuo you 傾身 qin shen 勢 shi	第一勢 di yi shi 托掌 tuo zhang 觀天 guan tian 勢 shi	預備勢 yu bei shi	張廣德 zhang guang de	引體令柔十三式 yin ti ling rou shi san shi

Thirteen Movements to Stretch the Body and Make it More Supple

Professor Zhang Guangde

Preparation

1. Push the hands upward, look at the sky
2. Lean the body to the left then to the right
3. Support the sky by turning the body
4. Open the chest by bending backwards
5. Bend the hips, lift the coccyx

第十三勢	第十二勢	第十一勢	第十勢	第九勢	第八勢	第七勢	第六勢
di shi san shi	di shi er shi	di shi yi shi	di shi shi	di jiu shi	di bas shi	di qi shi	di liu shi
zban chi tiao xi shi	zhi ti zhan li shi	qin ting bao zhu shi	ting xi diao wei shi	bai yuan suo shen shi	gong shen diao wei shi	diao wei you xuan shi	diao wei zuo xuan shi
展翅調息勢	直體站立勢	蜻蜓抱柱勢	挺膝吊尾勢	白猿縮身勢	躬身吊尾勢	吊尾右旋勢	吊尾左旋勢

6. Lift the coccyx and turn to the left
7. Lift the coccyx and turn to the right
8. Bend the hips, lift the coccyx
9. The white chimpanzee folds its body
10. Stretch the legs, lift the coccyx
11. The dragonfly embraces the column
12. Return to the standing position
13. Open the wings to regulate the breathing

MOVEMENT

PREPARATION

Movement

1. Stand upright; relax the entire body, legs straight, and the arms alongside the body. Keep the body upright, *Zhong Xian*.[5] Lightly close the mouth, raise the tongue and place the tip on the palate. Look ahead.

2. Cross the hands and place them on the zone of *Dan Tian*, the left hand below for both men and women. Concentrate the mind on *Qi Hai* CV6. Look ahead or slightly close the eyes, silently reciting the poem of preparation.

3. At the end of the poem, lower the arms alongside the body, Look ahead.

Key points

1. Lightly close the mouth and teeth.

2. When silently reciting the poem of the preparation, no sound at all should be heard.

---

5 中线 *Zhong Xian*, or for Buddhists, 中脉 *Zhong Mai* 'the central vertical axis'. *Zhong*: centre, the middle. *Xian*: the line, the thread. *Mai*: the meridian, the pulse. See Appendix 5, 'Thirteen Movements, Technical Considerations'. It involves correctly placing man in relation to the Sky and Earth. The correct posture makes it possible to establish this axis which facilitates the circulation of *Qi* between the Sky, Man and Earth. It is essential to find this most direct, shortest and simplest pathway of *Qi*. 'Find simplicity' is a great rule in Taoist physical practice.

6 *Dan Tian*: see Appendix 1.

7 *Que Qiao*: 'The Magpie Bridge'; see Appendix 2.

shen	身	hu	呼	yi	意	ye	夜
qing	輕	xi	吸	shou	守	lan	闌
ru	如	xu	徐	dan	丹	ren	人
yan	燕	huan	緩	tian	田	jing	靜
piao	飄	da	搭	feng	封	wan	萬
yun	雲	que	鵲	qi	七	lu	慮
xiao	霄	qiao	橋	qiao	竅	pao	抛

It grows dark; all is calm, silence.
Dismiss the ten thousand concerns of life.
Concentrate your mind in the *Dan Tian*,[6] the lower field of cinnabar
And fully close the seven openings of the face.
Breathe deeply, slowly, softly
Making the 'Magpie Bridge'.[7]
The body becomes light as a swallow in the springtime
Which swoops and soars towards the distant clouds.

FIRST MOVEMENT: PUSH THE HANDS UPWARD, LOOK AT THE SKY

托掌观天势 *Tuo Zhang Guan Tian Shi*

Movement

Elements 1, 2 and 3 are those of the preparation.

4. Following on from the preparation. Bring the hands in front of the stomach, and interlock the fingers, palms upwards. Look ahead. Keeping the hands close to the body, raise them level with the chest, then make an internal rotation of the hands, lift them to face level and then push them upward continuously. When the hands are fully raised, turn

the face upwards, and look at the back of the hands. The arms are extended, palms upwards. Hold this posture for a few moments, continuing to look upwards.

5. At the end of the required interval, without changing the body position, return the head to upright. Look ahead.

Key points

1. Relax the chest and keep the back straight, push the hands upwards with force. The arms are extended, but relax all the joints to the maximum extent so that they are neither stretched nor stiff. Breathe naturally.

2. After pushing the hands upwards, remain in position for several moments.

Action

1. Increases the ability to stretch and extend, treating curvature of the spine, pains in the neck, shoulders, elbows or wrists.

2. Regulates the Triple Heater[8] and frees the water passage.

---

8   *San Jiao Jing* signifies 'the Triple Heater meridian'. Its usual title is *Shou Shao Yang*, 'lesser *Yang* of the hand'. In English it is usually referred to as 'the Triple Heater meridian' and by convention the corresponding system which harmonises the function of all the organs is called the 'Three Burners'.

SECOND MOVEMENT: LEAN THE BODY TO THE LEFT THEN TO THE RIGHT

左右倾身势 *Zuo You Qin Shen Shi*

Movement

Keep the arms and the palms in the final position of the first movement.

1. Open the chest, lean the body to the left.

2. Open the chest, return to the upright position.

3. Open the chest, lean the body to the right.

4. Open the chest, return to the upright position.

Look forwards throughout this sequence.

Key points

1. The knees are extended. Keep the feet stable as if rooted in the earth, push the hands strongly upward. Lean the body the maximum possible to the left and right. The aged or frail should lean according to their ability and limits.

2. When leaning the body to the left and right, hold the position for several moments to obtain the best result.

3. The breathing must remain natural and unforced.

Action

1. Develops good flexibility and body resistance.

2. Increases the quality of balance and resistance strength.

3. Releases the three *Yin* and three *Yang* meridians of the hand as well as the gall bladder, liver, *Du Mai* and *Ren Mai* meridians.[9]

THIRD MOVEMENT: SUPPORT THE SKY WHILE TURNING THE BODY

托天旋转势 *Tuo Tian Xuan Zhuan Shi*

Movement

1. Following on from the preceding movement. Twist around the central axis to the left as much as possible, look behind and to the left.

2. Without changing the position of the hands, twist around the central axis towards the right to bring the body back to facing forwards. Look ahead.

3. Same as 1, but turning towards the right.

4. Same as 2, opposite direction.

Key points

1. Push *Bai Hui* upwards, open the chest; keep the back upright, the legs do not move. Push the hands upwards to the maximum extent, keeping the body completely vertical. The extent of the movement depends on the individual ability of the practitioner.

2. When the body twists to the left or right, hold the position for several moments at the maximum point of the movement.

3. Breathing must remain natural and unforced.

---

9   *Du Mai*, Governing Vessel, and *Ren Mai*, Conception Vessel.

Action

1. Frees both the small and large 'celestial cycles'.

2. Increases flexibility and resistance in the hip joints and the lumbar region.

3. Releases the three *Yin* and three *Yang* meridians of the foot.

FOURTH MOVEMENT: OPEN THE CHEST BY BENDING BACKWARDS

舒胸仰体势 *Shu Xiong Yang Ti Shi*

Movement

1. Continuing from the preceding position, with the knees straight, open the chest upwards, which stretches the stomach region, and lean backwards to the greatest degree possible, pushing the hands strongly upwards. Lift the face and look up.

2. Return the body to its upright position and look forwards again, still pushing the hands upwards.

Key points

1. Breathing must remain natural and unforced.

2. When leaning the body backwards, keep the knees straight. The toes must firmly grip the ground; the hands are pushed vertically upwards to keep the body solid and stable.

Action

1. Increases the suppleness of the muscles of the lumbar region, helps the articulation of the lumbar vertebrae, releasing stiffness in this zone.

2. Frees and circulates energy in the *Ren Mai* and *Du Mai* meridians to strengthen the kidneys and lumbar region and reinforce the *Yin* and the original energy.

FIFTH MOVEMENT: BEND THE HIPS, LIFT THE COCCYX

躬身吊尾势 *Gong Shen Diao Wei Shi*

Movement

Keeping the knees extended, raise the coccyx and fold the hips, lowering the upper body forwards. The hands touch the ground; gently raise the head. Look ahead.

Key points

1. The flexing and lowering of the upper body must be done slowly. Completely relax the muscles of the lumbar region, fold the hips, raise the coccyx and lift the head. For those suffering from high blood pressure, it is essential to raise the head and not lower the upper body too much.

2. If, as in the case of the elderly, frail or sick, the hands do not manage to touch the ground, the posture should not be forced. The essential factor is to keep the knees extended.

Action

1. Significantly harmonises the mobility and resistance of the lumbar vertebrae and the legs, in order to lubricate the joints and reduce stiffness.

2. Harmonises the movement of blood in the head, increases the pulmonary capacity.

SIXTH MOVEMENT: LIFT THE COCCYX AND TURN TO THE LEFT

吊尾左旋势 *Diao Wei Zuo Xuan Shi*

Movement

1. Following on from the preceding position, with the knees extended and the hands touching the ground, turn the upper body to slide the hands beside the left foot, lightly raising the head.

2. With the knees extended, slide the hands to bring them in front again, keeping the head lightly raised.

Key points

1. The breathing must remain natural and unforced.

2. The degree of rotation to the left must be the greatest possible for the individual, but the rhythm of this movement must remain slow, and completely without force.

Action

1. Increases the flexibility of rotation of the lumbar region and the hips, lubricates the joints and reduces stiffness.

2. Softens and releases the meridians throughout the body, frees the movement of blood and energy to treat and prevent lumbago, pain in the legs or pathologies in the zone of the kidneys and the bladder.

SEVENTH MOVEMENT: LIFT THE COCCYX AND TURN TO THE RIGHT

吊尾右旋势 *Diao Wei You Xuan Shi*

Movement

Continuing from the preceding position, with the knees extended and the hands touching the ground, turn the upper body to slide the hands beside the right foot, and lightly raise the head.

Key points

The same as those of the sixth movement.

Action

The same as those of the sixth movement.

EIGHTH MOVEMENT: BEND THE HIPS, LIFT THE COCCYX

躬身吊尾势 *Gong Shen Diao Wei Shi*

Movement

This movement is a transition between the seventh and the ninth movement.

Following on from the preceding movement, extend the knees, slide the hands on the ground to bring them back in front of the toes, raise the head. Thus, one returns to the position of the fifth movement 'Bend the hips, lift the coccyx'.

Key points

1. Breathe naturally, without forcing.

2. If, as in the case of the elderly, frail or sick, the hands do not manage to touch the ground, the posture should not be forced. The essential factor is to keep the knees extended.

Action

1. Noticeably improves the suppleness and resistance of the lumbar region and the legs, lubricating the joints and reducing stiffness.

2. Harmonises the movement of blood in the head, increases the pulmonary capacity.

NINTH MOVEMENT: THE WHITE CHIMPANZEE FOLDS ITS BODY

白猿缩身势 *Bai Yuan Suo Shen Shi*

Movement

Following on from the preceding movement. The fingers remain interlocked, firmly touching the ground. With knees touching each other, fold them, lowering the buttocks as far as possible without raising the heels. Lift the head and look into the distance.

Key points

1. Exhale as deeply as possible so that the thighs are well against the upper body.

2. If unable to squat completely, it is sufficient to half squat, but the heels must remain on the floor.

Action

1. Expels impurities to purify the lung.

2. Increases the flexibility of the joints throughout the body, lubricating them and reducing stiffness.

TENTH MOVEMENT: STRETCH THE LEGS, LIFT THE COCCYX

挺膝吊尾势 *Ting Xi Diao Wei Shi*

Movement

Following on from the preceding movement, with the hands touching the ground, raise the coccyx, fully straighten the legs, completely relax the lumbar region and the back; the toes solidly grip the ground. Lift the head and look forwards.

Key points

1. Following the extension of the legs, gently inhale and exhale completely; then continue breathing naturally.

2. This movement must be performed very slowly. It is essential to relax the muscles in the lumbar region and the hips, and to lightly raise the head.

Action

1. Good for developing the flexibility and coordination of the legs, knees, ankles and toes.

2. Lubricates the joints of the lumbar region, hips, knees and ankles, frees and invigorates the meridians, to encourage energy and blood to circulate.

ELEVENTH MOVEMENT: THE DRAGONFLY EMBRACES THE COLUMN

蜻蜓抱柱势 *Qin Ting Bao Zhu Shi*

Movement

Following on from the preceding movement, straighten the knees, separate the hands then grasp the legs, the tips of the middle fingers placed on *Tai Xi* Kid3, pull the chest and the belly towards the thighs, making the posture of the dragonfly embracing the column. Raise the head slightly.

Key points

1. Maintain natural breathing. Pause for several moments when grasping the legs.

2. The elderly, frail or ill, or those who may have difficulties grasping the legs, should perform this movement according to their capabilities; it is essential that those suffering from high blood pressure raise the head.

Action

1. Helps to reduce stiffness, particularly at the lumbar level and in the legs; lubricates the joints, reduces pain.

2. Strengthens the weaker parts of the body and consolidates the body as a whole; helps to eliminate lesions.

3. Releases *Du Mai* as well as the kidney, liver, spleen and bladder meridians; frees the liver, nourishes the muscles and tendons, reinforces the spleen, tones the muscles.

TWELFTH MOVEMENT: RETURN TO THE STANDING POSITION

直体站立势 *Zhi Ti Zhan Li Shi*

Movement

Following on from the preceding movement, with the knees still extended, slowly raise the upper body, the arms lowering alongside the body. Look ahead.

Key points

The head is the starting point for raising the upper body. Inhale during this extension, and look into the distance.

Action

Reinforces the lumbar region and the dorsal muscles.

THIRTEENTH MOVEMENT: OPEN THE WINGS TO REGULATE THE BREATHING

展翅调息势 *Zhan Chi Tiao Xi Shi*

Movement

1. Following on from the preceding movement, while inhaling, contract the anus, tighten the perineum, pushing *Bai Hui* upwards, using the entire body; with tension in the back of the wrists, raise the hands sideways to shoulder level, palms downward. Look ahead.

2. While exhaling, release the belly and anus, relax the body, fold the knees slightly, lowering the hands to the sides, as far as hip level, palms downward, the fingers towards the outside. Look ahead.

Repetitions

Perform the movement three times, each comprising one inhalation and one exhalation.

Key points

1. Relax the entire body; calm the mind and the emotions. The movement must be slow and harmonious, with fine and regular breathing.

2. Coordinate the movements of raising the arms, straightening the knees, folding the knees and lowering the arms, etc.

3. When the folding the knees, they should touch each other. When lowering the arms, it is essential first to relax and lower the shoulders, then lower the elbows, then the wrists and finally the hands, in order to bring energy to the *Dan Tian*.

Action

1. Restores the mind and the position of the body.

2. Increases the capacity of the heart and the lung, harmonises the emotions and releases tension.

CLOSING

1. Straighten the legs, bring the hands forwards, cross them and place them on the zone of *Dan Tian*, the left hand underneath for men, the right hand for women.[10] Look ahead.

2. Remain for a moment, then lower the arms alongside the body. Look forwards.

3. Rub the hands together three times, and then massage the face three times. Finally, lower the arms alongside the body, and bring the practice quietly to a close.

EXPLANATION

This sequence is a form of *Dao Yin* in which the movements relate to the meridians and it allows the body – mainly by the changes of position – to be consolidated, increasing its softness, flexibility, power and resistance.

For example:

---

10 During his lifetime, a man expends more energy whereas a woman expends more blood. This is why, at the end of the movement, men reinforce their energy by placing the left hand (*Yang*) on the zone of *Dan Tian* and women invigorate their blood by placing the right hand (*Yin*) on the zone of *Dan Tian*.

- Our arms are generally positioned alongside the body, but in this sequence, they must be raised to the maximum and kept for some time in that position.

- Generally speaking, the head marks the top of the body, but in this sequence, it is lowered as much as possible and the position maintained for some moments.

- The body is normally upright, but in this sequence, it is turned to the left, to the right, folded forward and backward to the greatest extent possible, using internal force.

- These kinds of characteristics are examples of 'associating movement and stillness, with the emphasis on stillness', and 'stretching, lengthening, using power in slowness'.

Thanks to these changes of body position, which promote the circulation of *Qi* and blood, the eight extraordinary and 12 principal meridians are cleared, and the five organs, six entrails, four limbs, hundred joints, the muscles and tendons, flesh and skin are all stimulated and protected.

These movements coordinate the balance between top and bottom, left and right, external and internal, and therefore *Yin* and *Yang*.

The sequence lubricates the joints, alleviates stiffness, frees adhesions, and relieves pains in the neck, shoulders, lumbar region and the four limbs, increasing the capacity of the body's defences.

ADDITIONAL DETAILS

1. The title of this form indicates that it is a sequence of stretching to make the body more flexible and more resistant. In principle, the exercise is more appropriate for young people, and in practice the elderly and sick (especially those with cardiac conditions and high blood

pressure) can reduce the degree of difficulty by reducing the extremity of the stretching.

2. This sequence is difficult: it includes many movements of folding, leaning, etc. and the degree of movement is extreme. For this reason it should be practised gradually, working within individual capabilities. Beginning with gentle movements, the appropriate level is gradually achieved.

3. This sequence can be linked with other sets of *Dao Yin Yang Sheng Gong*, but when linked with the sequence, 'Relax the Heart and Regulate the Blood', to respect that form's characteristic of softness, it is essential to decrease the degree of difficulty of the stretching.

4. Before practising this exercise, it is necessary generally to warm up the joints, muscles and the tendons.

5. As the degree of movement is strong, following the sequence, it is necessary to relax the body, using self-massage, gently striking the legs and the lumbar region.

6. The sequence can be linked with one of the *Yang Sheng Tai Ji* forms, providing mutual stimulation. It can also be used as a preparation in other sports.

7. This sequence is forbidden for pregnant women.

8. Refer also to the additional details for other sequences.

9. Best results are achieved when practising in a good mood, eliminating sudden changes of emotion.

PHOTOGRAPHS

Preparation

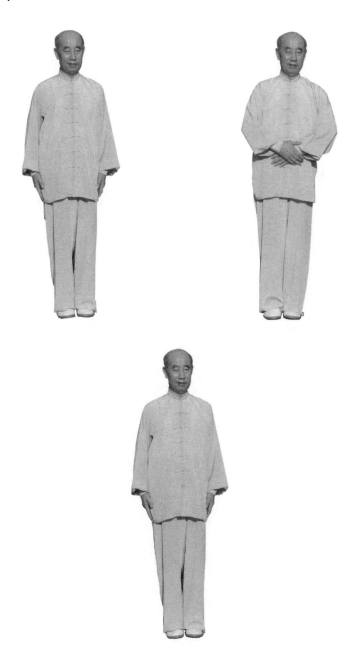

First movement: Push the hands upward, look at the sky

托掌观天势 *Tuo Zhang Guan Tian Shi*

Second movement: Lean the body to the left then to the right

左右倾身势 *Zuo You Qin Shen Shi*

Third movement: Support the sky while turning the body

托天旋转势 *Tuo Tian Xuan Zhuan Shi*

Fourth movement: Open the chest by bending backwards

舒胸仰体势 *Shu Xiong Yang Ti Shi*

Fifth movement: Bend the hips, lift the coccyx

躬身吊尾势 *Gong Shen Diao Wei Shi*

Sixth movement: Lift the coccyx and turn to the left

吊尾左旋势 *Diao Wei Zuo Xuan Shi*

Seventh movement: Lift the coccyx and turn to the right

吊尾右旋势 *Diao Wei You Xuan Shi*

Eighth movement: Bend the hips, lift the coccyx

躬身吊尾势 *Gong Shen Diao Wei Shi*

Ninth movement: The white chimpanzee folds its body

白猿缩身势 *Bai Yuan Suo Shen Shi*

Tenth movement: Stretch the legs, lift the coccyx

挺膝吊尾势 *Ting Xi Diao Wei Shi*

Eleventh movement: The dragonfly embraces the column

蜻蜓抱柱势 *Qin Ting Bao Zhu Shi*

Twelfth movement: Return to the standing position

直体站立势 *Zhi Ti Zhan Li Shi*

Thirteenth movement: Open the wings to regulate the breathing

展翅调息势 *Zhan Chi Tiao Xi Shi*

Closing

PART 2

Guiding and Harmonising Energy to Regulate the Breath

導氣令和調息功

Dao Qi Ling He
Tiao Xi Gong

INTRODUCTION

This form is an important part of *Dao Yin Yang Sheng Gong*; it can be used as a basis of *Dao Yin Yang Sheng*, of *Yang Sheng Tai Ji*, or as a preparation for all the sequences, as well as an entirely separate method for reinforcing the health, and preventing and treating various chronic illnesses.

The word *Dao Yin* is found for the first time in the *Zhuang Zi* in the chapter (*Ke Yi*) where it says, 'To attain longevity, inhale, exhale; eject the old, ingest the new; imitate the bear which stretches its spine and the bird which extends its neck and wings.'

Definitions of *Dao Yin* vary in the ancient texts.

From *Cheng Yuan Ying*: 'Exhale cold breath in order to get rid of the old, inhale warm breath to assimilate the new, imitate the bear which clings to the trees, and the bird which flies while stretching its legs.'

From *Li Yi*: 'guiding the energy makes it flow smoothly: stretching the body makes it supple'. He considers that it is a method for health that links breathing and movement of the body. It is a type of moving *Qi Gong*.

But in these ancient documents these kinds of explanations remain very general, without drawings or text to accompany them. To make this practice available to the general public, so people can maintain their health, Professor Zhang's study of ancient *Dao Yin* has enabled him to create this sequence based on the theory of the *Yi Jing* and Chinese traditional medicine.

CHARACTERISTICS

Its principal characteristics are:

- movements that are easy, simple, comfortable and pleasant

- calmness and movement are linked

- an emphasis on calmness.

The form is composed of three movements:

1. Regulate the breathing on the left.

2. Regulate the breathing on the right.

3. Regulate the breathing on both sides.

MOVEMENT (STANDING)

shou 收 shi 勢	di 第 san 三 shi 勢 shuan 雙 tiao 調 xi 息	di 第 er 二 shi 勢 you 右 tiao 調 xi 息	di 第 yi 一 shi 勢 zuo 左 tiao 調 xi 息	yu 預 bei 備 shi 勢	zhang 張 guang 廣 de 德	dao 導 qi 氣 ling 令 he 和 tiao 調 xi 息 gong 功
Guiding and harmonising energy to regulate the breath Professor Zhang Guangde Preparation 1. Regulate the breathing on the left 2. Regulate the breathing on the right 3. Regulate the breathing on both sides Closing						

PREPARATION

Movement

1. Stand upright; relax the entire body; find the vertical axis and keep the body upright, the arms by the sides. Raise the

tongue and place the tip on the palate; Look forward or slightly close the eyes.[11]

2. Move the body weight onto the right foot, slightly bend the right knee; step sideways to the left to shoulder width, the toes forward. Look ahead. Then, move the body weight between the feet, straightening the knees, and keeping the body upright. Continue to look ahead.

3. Lower the hands, cross them and place them on the zone of *Qi Hai*[12] CV4, the left hand below for both men and women.[13] Concentrate the mind on *Qi Hai*. Look ahead or slightly close the eyes, silently reciting the poem of preparation.

---

11 The gaze is important in the practice of *Dao Yin*; it indicates the state of mind of the practitioner. 'Look forward' refers both to the correct position of the head and an image of freedom (looking into the distance). On the other hand, 'slightly close the eyes' is a method of concentrating, bringing the gaze to the interior. When the text indicates, 'look forward', 'slightly close the eyes' as well, except at the end of the whole sequence.

12 *Qi Hai* forms part of *Dan Tian*. See Appendix 1.

13 The left hand is the *Yang* side linked with energy, movement; the right hand is the *Yin* side linked with blood, calmness. During the preparation, to begin the movement, first the side associated with movement is stimulated, thus it is the left hand that is underneath and touches the *Dan Tian* for both men and women.

shen	身	hu	呼	yi	意	ye	夜
qing	輕	xi	吸	shou	守	lan	闌
ru	如	xu	徐	dan	丹	ren	人
yan	燕	huan	緩	tian	田	jing	靜
piao	飄	da	搭	feng	封	wan	萬
yun	雲	que	鵲	qi	七	lu	慮
xiao	霄	qiao	橋	qiao	竅	pao	拋

It grows dark, all is calm, silent.
Dismiss the ten thousand concerns of life.
Concentrate your mind on *Dan Tian*,[14] the lower field of cinnabar
And fully close the seven openings of the face.
Breathe deeply, slowly, softly
Making the 'Magpie Bridge'.[15]
The body becomes light as the swallow in springtime
Which swoops and soars towards the distant clouds.

Key points

1. Lightly close the mouth.

2. At the end of the recitation, lower the arms alongside the body.

---

14 *Dan Tian*: see Appendix 1.
15 *Que Qiao*: 'The Magpie Bridge': see Appendix 2

FIRST MOVEMENT: REGULATE THE BREATHING ON THE LEFT

左调息 *Zuo Tiao Xi*

Movement

1. Inhaling, contract *Gu Dao*,[16] tighten the perineum, straighten the knees; at the same time, following an internal rotation of the arms, raise them sideways, making an angle of 60° with the body, palms backwards, arms extended. Look ahead then, using an external rotation of the arms, turn the palms forwards. Continue to look ahead.

2. Exhaling, relax the belly and *Gu Dao*. Bend the knees slightly, relax the entire body; relax the lumbar region; draw in the buttocks in order to release the heart and chest, *Xin Xiong*;[17] bring the right hand to the waist on the right, thumb toward the back; place the left *Lao Gong* HP8 on *Guan Yuan* CV4. Use fine, regular, long and deep abdominal breathing. Look ahead.

Key points

1. Concentrate the mind, release the chest and the heart, coordinate thought and breathing, eliminate unwanted thoughts.

2. Relax the lower back, draw in the buttocks and relax the entire body. The extent of the movements of the belly

---

16 *Gu Dao*: 'the pathway of cereals (food)', which may also be called *Po Men*, the anus.

17 *Xin Xiong* 心胸. *Xin*: heart. *Xiong*: chest. In Chinese culture the word chest is very often linked with the word heart, because it is considered that the chest is the residence of the heart (physically and psychologically). In order to open the chest, the mind, and therefore the heart, must be freed. Conversely, when the mind is tense, the chest will be constricted.

during breathing (inflating/deflating) must be as great as possible, but made in a natural way, without forcing. Inhale pure air through the nose; expel impure air through the mouth. It is essential to produce this regular, deep, slow and fine breathing continuously.

3. Lower the pelvis when folding the knees. The level of descent depends on individual ability.

Length of practice

1 to 3 minutes.

Action

1. A book of Chinese traditional medicine says, 'To develop energy, it is first necessary to work on the concentration and the mastery of your thoughts' and 'Coordination between the thought and breathing makes it possible to lead energy by means of the mind' and further, 'Blood is the mother of energy and energy is the general [guide] of blood; when energy circulates, blood circulates; on the other hand blockages of energy result in the stagnation of blood.' This shows that the vital relationship between the mind and energy, enables the release of the meridians, and harmonises blood and energy to consolidate the body and treat disorders.

2. This movement permits the rapid establishment of a better and more balanced mental state, the elimination of unwanted thoughts and improved body coordination, in order to prevent and treat various disorders.

SECOND MOVEMENT: REGULATE THE BREATHING ON THE RIGHT

右调息 *You Tiao Xi*

Movement

1. Continuing from the preceding movement. Inhaling, contract the anus and the perineum, push *Bai Hui* GV20 upward, straighten the knees; following an internal rotation, raise the arms sideways until they form an angle of 60° with the body, palms backwards. Extend the arms, then, using an external rotation, turns the palms forwards. Look ahead.

2. Exhaling, relax the belly and the anus, slightly bend the knees, bring the left hand to the waist on the left, thumb towards the back and place the right *Lao Gong* on *Guan Yuan*. Use fine, regular, long and deep abdominal breathing. Look ahead or slightly close the eyes.

Key points

As in the previous movement.

Length of practice

1 to 3 minutes.

Action

As in the previous movement.

THIRD MOVEMENT: REGULATE THE BREATHING ON BOTH SIDES

双调息 *Shuan Tiao Xi*

Movement

1. Continuing from the previous movement, inhaling, contract the anus and perineum, straighten the knees; straighten the arms and following an internal rotation, raise them sideways until they form an angle of 60° with the body, palms facing backwards. Look forwards. Then, using an external rotation of the arms, turn the palms forwards. Continue to look forwards.

2. Exhaling, relax the belly and the anus. Bend the knees slightly, and make an external rotation of the arms, then bring the hands in front of the belly as if carrying a ball of energy between the hands and the belly. Then cross the hands and place them on the zone of *Guan Yuan*, the left hand below for men, the right hand for women.[18] Use fine, long, deep and regular abdominal breathing. Look ahead.

Key points

1. Calm the mind and the breathing. Harmonise the energy and relax the entire body.

---

18 The left hand is the *Yang* side linked with energy, and movement; the right hand is the *Yin* side linked with blood and calmness. Throughout life men expend more energy and women expend more blood. This is why men place the left hand on the zone of *Dan Tian* to fortify their energy, while women place their right hand on the zone of *Dan Tian* to invigorate their blood.

2. In calmness, find movement. This relationship circulates energy to free the meridians.

3. Gather energy, swallow saliva and direct them to *Dan Tian*.

Length of practice

1 to 3 minutes.

Action

1. Reinforces *Yuan Qi*[19] (original energy), strengthens the body, eliminates perverse energy.[20]

2. Calms the mind, brings peace to the heart, regulates *Yin* and *Yang*.

3. Releases and invigorates the meridians, regulates and harmonises energy and blood.

---

19 *Yuan Qi* 元气: original energy. *Yuan*: origin, source. *Qi*: energy. It is called original because it is the origin of the activity and the dynamic of all the organs and entrails and the body as a whole. This is why, in the Chinese tradition, the vitality of life is founded on this energy. When people age it is said that their *Yuan Qi* has weakened, and when they die that their *Yuan Qi* has become exhausted and disappeared. It is stored principally in the *Dan Tian*, then circulates and diffuses throughout the entire body. This is why, in the practice of *Dao Yin* from the preparation phase to the end, we must work to improve *Yuan Qi*. This is the shortest route and most effective method to improve our capacity for self healing.

20 *Xie Qi* 邪气: perverse energy. *Xie*: incorrect, deviant, that which is outside the correct path, perverse. *Qi*: energy. This perverse energy (either of internal or external origin) is regarded in Chinese medicine as one of the causes of illness.

CLOSING

Movement

1. Straighten the legs; lower the arms alongside the body. Look ahead.

2. Move the body weight onto the right foot; bring the left foot to the right, keeping the body upright. Look ahead.

3. Rub the hands three times; massage the face three times.

4. Quietly conclude the sequence.

MOVEMENT (SEATED)

1. Seated on a stool at knee height, place the feet firmly on the floor. Open the feet to shoulder width, toes forwards. Place the hands on the knees, *Lao Gong* on *Fu Tu* St32 and slightly close the eyes.

2. Cross the hands and place them on the zone of *Dan Tian*, the left hand below for both men and women.

3. Silently recite the poem of the preparation.

4. At the end, place the hands on the knees, *Lao Gong* on *Fu Tu* and slightly close the eyes.

Perform the movements as in the standing version but without moving the legs.

EXPLANATION

1. Thanks to the fine, regular, deep and slow abdominal breathing, the power of the diaphragm is increased, and the function of the lungs improved. More pure air is inhaled, more impure air exhaled.

2. This kind of abdominal breathing increases the amplitude of the diaphragm.[21] The spleen, the stomach, liver, gall bladder and the intestines are dynamically massaged. The circulation of energy and blood is stimulated, the secretion of gastric juice is increased and digestion and assimilation are made easier. Stagnation of blood in the zone of the liver is eliminated.

3. According to recent statistics, more than half of illnesses are due to functional disorders of the neurovegetative system. This method of breathing contributes to the regulation of the neurovegetative system, stimulates and controls the sympathetic and parasympathetic nervous systems in order to create balance in the body.

Abdominal respiration is a way of expending less energy while obtaining maximum results.

The respiratory system can be separated into two parts:

1. The system of the trachea, including the nose and the micro bronchi; this system does not have the function of exchanging the air between the body and nature, it is simply the pathway for air entering the body. This is why it is called 'the tube', without effect on breathing.

2. The organ of the lungs, which is composed of approximately 7.5 billion alveoli. This is the true place of the exchange of air.

---

21 See Appendix 6.

With each breath, air initially passes through the first zone, where there is no exchange function and fills it before arriving at the lung. The volume of useable air for breathing is the total volume of air inspired less the volume of the trachea.

This is why in a given period of time, fine, deep, long and regular abdominal breathing draws in much more useful air than superficial breathing can. It is therefore a breathing method expending less while being more effective.

ADDITIONAL DETAILS

1. Pay attention to maintaining a good body posture in both the standing and seated position. Lean neither to the right nor left. In the seated position, do not touch the back of the chair.

2. Relaxing the entire body is extremely important, because this makes it possible to establish a comfortable position, which in turn promotes stable, balanced and quiet breathing. In its turn such breathing enables the normal movement of rising and descent of energy, which supports the free circulation of energy and blood.

3. The importance of abdominal breathing cannot be overemphasised. According to individual ability, one of two methods can be chosen: Inhaling draw in the belly, or inhaling inflate the belly. In both methods, inhale and exhale through the nose, or inhale through the nose, exhale by the mouth, without sound or undue effort.

4. In this practice, the mind and the attention are concentrated in the *Dan Tian* (mainly *Qi Hai*, *Guan Yuan* and the navel), in order to eliminate unwanted thoughts. *Can Tong Qi*, an ancient book concerned with practices to enable the manufacture of internal cinnabar, says that, 'The ear, the eye and the mouth are three treasures that should be closed rather than opened. *Zhen Ren* (a high level Taoist sage) withdrew and hid at the bottom of a valley, floating and swimming quietly.' This indicates that, during our practice, it is necessary to close the mouth and eyes slightly, paying no attention to sounds, enabling a continuous concentration on *Dan Tian*.[22]

5. Regularity of breathing can be linked with the method known as *Tu Yin* (emitting a sound). In a book from the Sui Period entitled, *The Great Principles Of Chan Zhi Quan*, the great Buddhist *Qi Gong* master of the tian tai zong school said, 'The wise ones understood the correspondence of sounds with the organs: *Ke* with the heart, *Fu* with the kidney, *Xu* with the liver when there is heat in this zone, *Xi* with the triple heater when there are blockages in this zone.' Taking account of his state of health, the practitioner can choose the corresponding sound. However, when practising *Tu Yin* the sound itself must be internal; it should not be heard on the outside.

6. Link the concentration and the control of thoughts with energy. Concentrating and controlling the thoughts will guide the circulation of energy in a peaceful and balanced way. Both are valuable in finding calmness, and have the

---

22 The technique of abdominal respiration, in particular reverse abdominal respiration, linked with concentrating the mind, enables sensations to appear in the zone of *Dan Tian*. Practice over a long period enables the development of this sensation and enlarges this zone, which is the origin of the internal and external movements of the body (see *Yuan Qi* note 19, page 58).

effect of strengthening the body, through prevention and care.

7. Benefit from the effects of combining *Jing*, calm and *Dong*, movement. This sequence links calmness and movement, but emphasises calmness, in order to nourish energy. Calmness (*Jing*) brings peace to the heart, and thus facilitates the regulation of breathing. Movement (*Dong*) appears in changes of posture. These movements are simple and straightforward. This type of movement makes it possible to be comfortable, and to coordinate breathing, mind and posture.

8. This sequence which is based on calmness can be combined with other sequences of *Dao Yin Yang Sheng Gong* which are based on movement, such as another foundation sequence of *Dao Yin Yang Sheng Gong* or with one of the methods of ancient *Dao Yin – Ba Duan Jin, Yi Jin Jing, Wu Qin Xi*. This partnership creates a dynamic between *Jing* (calm) and *Dong* (movement), and between *Yin* and *Yang* to obtain the fullest internal (working with energy) and external (working on the muscles, tendons, bones and skin) effects.

9. The practice area should be flat, and in a calm, pleasant, clean and beautiful environment, with pure air.

10. To control and master the emotions is important in maintaining health, but not always easy. The practice alone of *Dao Yin* without the control of the emotions in everyday life is not sufficient. It is absolutely necessary to link the practice of *Dao Yin* with balancing the emotions in everyday life to achieve physical and mental health.

11. It is necessary to free the mind, to practise in a state of tranquillity and serenity, without striving for results, without impatience or haste.

12. You must have confidence; these exercises can regulate both the mind and the body. Establishing a state of calm is the basis for strengthening and healing the body.

13. You must persevere: 'it is no use fishing for three days and then leaving the net out to dry in the sun for two days'; it is continuous practice that brings results.

14. The saliva that accumulates in the mouth during practice should always be swallowed.

15. It is a good idea to choose the most appropriate time to practise, the morning being preferable. Do not practise if you are hungry or if you have over-eaten. Wear comfortable, loose clothing.

16. To be most effective, 30 minutes practice is recommended.

PHOTOGRAPHS

Preparation

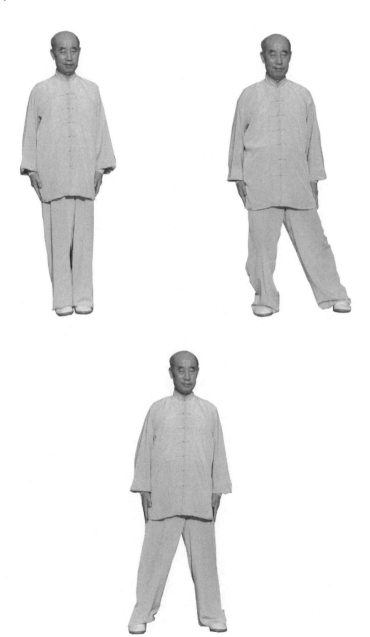

First movement: Regulate the breathing on the left

左调息 *Zuo Tiao Xi*

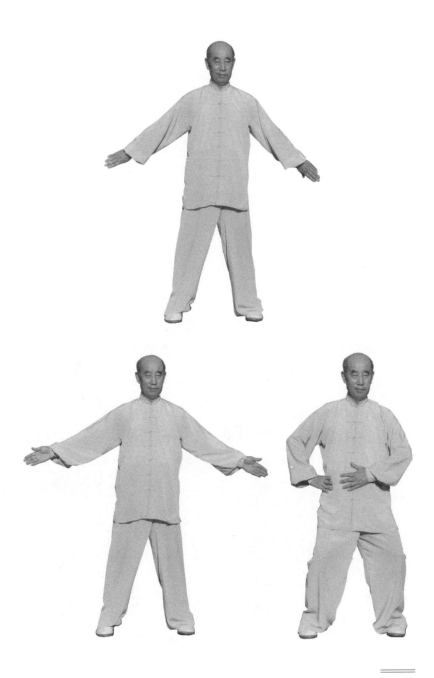

Second movement: Regulate the breathing on the right

右调息 *You Tiao Xi*

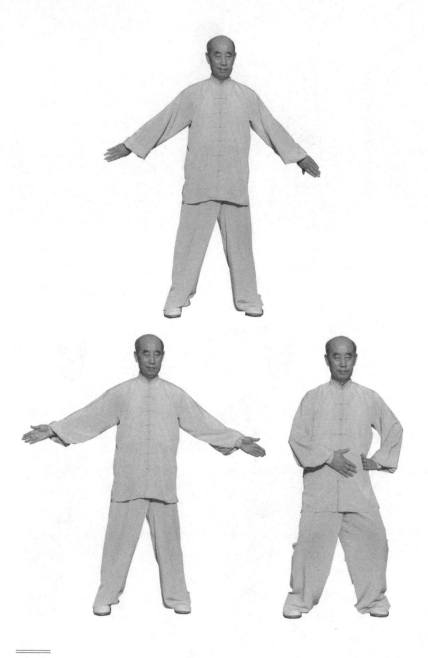

Third movement: Regulate the breathing on both sides

双调息 *Shuan Tiao Xi*

Closing

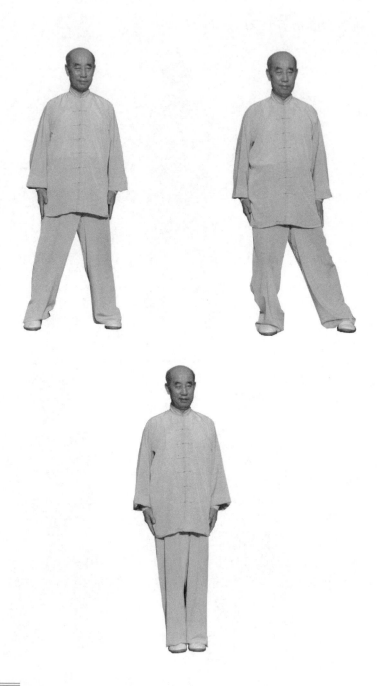

MASSAGING THE FACE

APPENDIX 1

Dan Tian 丹田
The Cinnabar Field

The first reference to *Dan Tian* is found in the *Huang Ting Jing* (*The Classic of the Central Yellow Palace*), a Taoist book of the Han Period concerning the practice of manufacturing internal cinnabar, in which it says:

There are three *Dan Tian* in the body:

The higher *Dan Tian*, which is also called *Ni Wan*, meaning 'clay ball'. This is the brain.

The middle *Dan Tian*, which is also called *Jiang Gong*, 'the crimson palace'. This is inside the chest, in the centre of the breast at the level of *Tan Zhong* CV17.

The lower *Dan Tian* is also called 'the palace of the subtle essence'. It is found 3 cun[23] below the navel, inside the pelvis at the level of *Qi Hai* CV6.

Dan Tian, especially the lower *Dan Tian*, is used in *Yang Sheng Tai Ji* and *Dao Yin*. The character *Tian* means a field; it is therefore not a point, but a zone found below the navel and includes most of the pelvis where the following points are located: *Shen Que, Tian Shu, Qi Hai Guan Yuan* and *Ming Men*.

---

23 *Cun*: a measure of length for locating acupuncture points. This is a personal measure and is different for each individual. 3 cun equals the width of four fingers.

- *Shen Que*: CV8 'the door of the spirit'. Found in the centre of the navel, the centre of the earth; it represents the source of 'after-heaven' *Qi*.

- *Tian Shu*: St25 'the celestial pivot'. Situated 2 cun each side of the navel, it is the mu point of the large intestine, located on the path of the stomach meridian, related to the earth. It regulates the movement of rising and descending between heaven and earth, and thus connects posterior (acquired) and anterior (innate) energy.

- *Qi Hai*: CV6 'the ocean of energy'. 1.5 cun below *Shen Que*. It stores subtle essences and original energy.

- *Guan Yuan*: CV4 'the barrier[24] of original energy'. Located 3 cun below the navel. It is the mu point of the small intestine, therefore the place of fire and warming. It is the crossing point of the three *Yin* meridians of the foot – liver, spleen and kidney – with the Conception Vessel. It is in this place that original energy is stored.

- *Ming Men*: GV4 'the door of life'. Located between the two kidneys, therefore fire is found surrounded by water. *Ming Men* has the function of heating the water of the kidneys, and transforming the *Jing* (the 'subtle essence') of the kidneys into *Yuan Qi*: life.

To sum up, the zone of *Dan Tian* contains the spleen and stomach, which constitute a large part of the posterior source. In addition, it contains the original energy and the function of reinforcing the fire of the kidney, which constitute the greater part of the anterior source. This is why the zone of *Dan Tian* is the place of

---

24 Barrier, in this context it is a place of passage (a turnstile rather than a barricade).

transformation between the subtle essence and the energy, and is therefore the basis of energy transformation. This is why *Dao Yin* exercises begin and end with the hands on *Dan Tian.*

It is desirable to experience a feeling of warmth in this zone when starting and ending the practice of *Dao Yin.*

APPENDIX 2

Que Qiao 鹊桥
The 'Magpie Bridge'

Q*ue Qiao* refers to a popular Chinese story: the herdsman and the weaver.

The Celestial Emperor had seven daughters, but his favourite was the youngest. She was very beautiful and industrious, which is why she was called Zhi Nu: *Zhi* meaning to weave and *Nu* indicating a girl. She worked unceasingly at her weaving.

One day, through her window, she saw a handsome young man on the Earth working the soil with oxen. He was called Niu Lang: *Niu* meaning ox, *Lang* indicating a boy. Zhi Nu fell in love with Niu Lang and, without asking her father's permission, she descended to Earth, and married him. They were very happy, and had two children, a boy and a girl.

Several years spent on Earth are equal to only a few days in heaven. The Celestial Emperor, not seeing his beloved daughter for a 'few days', searched for her and saw her on the Earth. He became very angry and sent the celestial army to bring her back. The chief of the army violently removed Zhi Nu, separating her from her husband and children. Niu Lang took a yoke, hung a basket at each end and put one of his children in each basket. Then he ran as quickly as he could to catch up with Zhi Nu, but he could not cross *Ying He*, the river of stars.

They remained separated from each other, one on each bank.

Hearing the children crying and the couple calling sadly to each other, many magpies came together and formed a bridge, allowing the couple to meet. But the Celestial Emperor allowed this reunion to take place only once a year, on 15 July of the Chinese calendar.

From that day, *Que Qiao* has become the symbol of a happy meeting.

In *Dao Yin* 'to raise the magpie bridge', means to raise the tongue, the tip touching the palate. This practice supports the connection, the happy meeting, of the upper ends of *Du Mai*, the *Yang* meridian and *Ren Mai*, the *Yin* meridian.

APPENDIX 3

Massaging the Face

The face massage comes at the end of the four basic sequences of preparation as well as at the end of many sequences in *Dao Yin Yang Sheng Gong*.

It is a method of calming the mind and effectively lowering energy to the zone of *Dan Tian*.

THE METHOD OF MASSAGE

Inhaling, place the fleshy part of the tips of the middle fingers in the hollow of the chin, at the point *Cheng Jiang* CV24. Massage around the mouth as far as *Ying Xiang* LI20; move up along the nose; pass through the *Jing Ming* BI1 points, then through *Zan Zhu* BI2 as far as *Shen Ting* GV24 and slide the hands to each side of the brow.

Exhaling, massage the sides of the brow, the temples, the cheeks, the jaw and return to the hollow of the chin.

Repeat this massage three times, then cross the hands and place them on the surface of *Dan Tian*, the left hand below for men, the right hand below for women. Remain for a moment in this posture then lower the arms alongside the body.

Why perform this massage three times?

In Chinese culture, numbers always have important significance. Three has various connotations, as outlined below.

YI SAN WEI BEN 以三为本: THREE IS THE ROOT OF UNDERSTANDING

The character *Wang* 王 is composed of the figure three 三, three lines connected by a vertical line. The three horizontal lines have a particular significance:

- the top line represents Heaven

- the middle line represents Man

- the bottom line represents the Earth.

To be able to govern a country it is necessary to understand perfectly these three parts.

YI SAN WEI DUO 以三为多: THREE INDICATES THE NUMEROUS

A single character 木 *Mu* can signify a tree or plank; two of them, 林 *Lin*, means a wood, or a small forest and three of them, 森 *Sen*, a large forest.

A single character 水 *Shui* can mean water; two characters (one the key 氵 and one *Shui* 水) gives the character *Yong* 泳, which means to swim, while three of them, 淼, gives *Miao* which, although not often used, means vast in regard to an expanse of water.

The single character *Huo* 火 indicates fire, two 炎 *Yan* (second tone) means to ignite and three 焱 *Yan* (fourth tone) flames.

YI SAN WEI ZUN 以三为尊: THREE SIGNIFIES RESPECT

During a wedding, the betrothed bow three times: to heaven, to the earth and to the parents.

When knocking on a door, it is disrespectful to knock more than three times.

YI SAN WEI XIAN 以三为限: THREE SIGNIFIES THE LIMIT

There is a Chinese proverb that says, 'Never make the same mistake three times.'

APPENDIX 4

Acupoints Used in the Foundation Sequences

Bai Hui	百会	GV20
Chang Qiang	長強	GV1
Cheng Jiang	承漿	CV24
Fu Tu	伏兔	St32
Ge Shu	膈俞	Bl17
Guan Yuan	关元	CV4
Hui Yin	会阴	CV1
Jia Ji	夾脊	See Appendix 4, 1.2
Jin Jin	金津	Extra 10, under the tongue on the left
Jing Ming	睛明	Bl1
Lao Gong	劳宫	HP8
Ming Men	命門	GV4
Qi Hai	气海	CV6
Shen Que	神阙	CV8
Shen Ting	神庭	GV24
Shen Shu	肾俞	Bl23
Su Liao	素	GV25

Tao Dao	陶道	GV13
Tan Zhong	膻中	CV17
Tian Shu	天枢	St25
Xuan Shu	懸樞	GV5
Ying Tang	印堂	Extra 1
Ying Xiang	迎香	LI20
Yong Quan	涌泉	Kid1
Yu Ye	玉液	Extra 10, under the tongue on the right
Yu Zhen	玉枕	Bl9
Zan Zhu	攢竹	Bl2
Zhi Yang	至陽	GV9
Zhong Wan	中脘	CV12

APPENDIX 5

Thirteen Movements, Technical Considerations

André Perret

PREPARATION: *ZHONG JIAN* 中线 THE CENTRAL VERTICAL AXIS

This preparation is common to all sequences of *Dao Yin Yang Sheng Gong*. Abdominal breathing and the necessary relaxation are described in all the sequences. The basic posture: 'standing upright, feet together, between heaven and earth, establish a vertical position' often raises difficulties. These vary from one person to another; awareness of them and their correction depends on the sensations experienced.

The greatest difficulty is to stand upright, tall but at the same time relaxed. It is essential that in wanting to make yourself taller, not to become tense; in wanting to relax, not to become limp.

The technique required to achieve consists of pressing on the ground in order to root the feet, while simultaneously pushing the top of the head (*Bai Hui* GV20, at the point equidistant between the ears) upward in order to lengthen the body as standing against a measuring apparatus, or as if lifting a weight balanced on the head. This enables the natural stretching of the spinal column and reduces thoracic and lumbar cervical curves, as well as relaxing the shoulders. Thus, 'Man between Heaven and Earth is great' (*Lao*

Zi). The correct posture enables the creation of this axis, which facilitates the circulation of *Qi* between Heaven, Man and Earth.

This correct circulation of *Qi* is only possible through control of the three barriers,[25] *San Guan* 三關: *Wei Lu Guan* at the level of the coccyx, *Jia Ji Guan* between the shoulder blades and *Yu Zhen Guan* at the level of the nape of the neck. These three barriers are places of control, mastery and filtration. They must be free of any obstacle in order to allow the free circulation of *Yang* energy.

Gaining control of the movement is not obvious for many beginners. To help them, it is possible to use complementary exercises to identify specific sensations.

Earth: the lower limbs

THE KNEES

The knees must be relaxed, very slightly bent, i.e. they are not at their maximum extension. In *Dao Yin Yang Sheng Gong*, when the leg (or the elbow) is extended, it is always necessary to keep a very light inflection, a reserve of extension, in the knee (or the elbow) in order for energy to circulate. To establish this, first push the knees backwards until feeling a posterior tension, then push them very slightly forward until that feeling disappears. If you bend them too much, an anterior tension begins to appear, and then it is necessary to move them back a little again until there is an absence of tension in the knees. This absence of tension is the key to a good posture and the efficient circulation of *Qi*.

THE FEET

The feet are together, but it is necessary to try to feel the pressure on the ground well distributed, not just on the heels but also on the front part of the sole and the toes. To do this, rock the body very

---

25 The three barriers are described in Appendix 4 in Volume 1 on the Small Celestial Cycle.

slightly back and forth through the ankle to discover the position where you feel the weight is best distributed. Rock slightly back to feel the support on the heels, then rock forwards to feel the support on the forefoot. In this exercise the body should not be bent in any way, the movement being contained in the ankle.

This exercise is important because it is used naturally in the movements of *Dao Yin*: when the body is lowered, initially the pressure will be on the heels, when rising, initially it will be in the forefoot and the toes. This slight rocking at the level of ankle is the root of stability and the roundness of the movements of *Dan Tian*, *Ming Men*, of the waist, and the entire body.

The posture is correct when the support is felt equally on the heels and the forefoot. This is essential for the good practice of the 13 movements and, generally speaking, is sufficient. But the sensation of rooting can be further improved by pressing the toes on the ground and by slightly clenching the front part of the feet, without raising them from the ground. This pressure must be very light in order not to create other tensions in the body, but nevertheless sufficient to support the good posture of the knees and the pelvis. It makes it possible to feel the rooting sensation in the entire foot and at the same time to form a light hollow in the area of *Yong Quan* Kid1. This feeling is the key to gathering the *Yin* energy of the earth.

Man: the trunk

THE PELVIS AND LUMBAR REGION

The correct position of the pelvis requires us to 'draw in the buttocks' while 'relaxing the lumbar region'. But equally it is necessary to keep the body and the head upright, without bending the back, or pushing the hips forward.

Mobilising the pelvis requires the conscious action of pushing the first barrier, *Wei Lu Guan*,[26] i.e. the point of the coccyx. This is a movement of retroversion (tilting the pelvis backwards) around the hips: the feeling experienced is that the coccyx slides downwards, forwards a little, then upwards (describing a small arc). At the same time, this movement involves a light pulling back of the navel, perceived by the hand placed on *Dan Tian*, and a stretching in the lumbar region is also felt. Lumbar lordosis (arching in the lower back) decreases or disappears.

Some people have never experienced this movement. To become aware of it, first it is necessary to practise the opposite movement, moving back the coccyx, 'pushing out the buttocks', then gradually bringing the coccyx gently forwards again, 'drawing in the buttocks', first to their natural position, then trying to continue beyond. With a little practice, awareness of this movement leads to being able to control it directly. With the legs extended, this movement is slight, but it is made easier by the very slight bending of the knees.

In *Dao Yin* the postures always begin with this movement which involves a feeling of fullness in the lumbar region, in particular at the level of *Ming Men* GV4 and *Shen Shu* Bl 23, and also a feeling of heaviness, of presence in the lower belly – *Dan Tian*. This feeling is the key to a good posture for the activation of *Qi.*

In the 13 movements, ensure that this retroversion of the pelvis is maintained in all the postures and in particular during the stretching of the upper body with the arms upwards. Each intermediate posture allows for this essential control, so that the next stretching takes place in a good position. At no time should the buttocks alone be pushed outwards; indeed, even when required to raise the coccyx in order to fold the hips, the entire trunk is involved in the movement; the lower back should not be arched.

---

26 *Wei Lu Guan* 尾呂關. *Wei*: the tail. *Lu*: the name of a Chinese minority living at the mouth of a river. It carries the notion of a mouth, of the link between water and the skeletal system. This refers to the tip of the coccyx, the mouth of a river that descends from Mount *Kun Lun* (i.e. the top of the skull).

THE THORAX AND THE BACK

The trunk is straight and relaxed. The chest should be neither inflated nor collapsed. Many people are naturally stooped: they present a thoracic hyper-kyphosis (curvature of the spine) that is either irreversible (problems of growth, vertebral compression, etc.) or reversible, being related to postural habits, or more often to anxiety, tiredness or depression. This hyper-kyphosis limits the thoracic movements and often causes painful cervical, scapular, thoracic or lumbar tension, or tension in the arms. Thoracic breathing aggravates these tensions and also decreases the mobility of the thoracic vertebrae. It is essential to replace it with abdominal breathing.

In every case, it should be accepted that the movement of the thoracic zone is limited to some extent. But, while respecting these limits, progressive improvements are always possible. Thus, while the preparation posture will not be perfect in the beginning, it will nevertheless be more correct than someone's habitual posture, and it will improve gradually with practice.

It is important to free the middle thoracic zone, in particular between the seventh and eighth thoracic vertebrae in order to move it consciously. At this level, at the height of the tips of the shoulder blades, is the second barrier: *Jia Ji Guan*.[27] The conscious mobilisation of this zone is difficult at the beginning; it can be isolated by preparatory exercises of opening and closing the chest. To close the chest: *Jia Ji Guan* moves back and draws *Tan Zhong* CV17 backwards, the chest hollows and the nipples approach. To open the chest: *Jia Ji Guan* pushes *Tan Zhong* CV17 forwards and the nipples separate. This movement can be controlled by placing the hands on the breasts, the tips of the middle fingers touching

---

27 *Jia Ji Guan* 夾脊關. *Jia*: to close, pinch, grip. *Ji*: the spine, the vertebrae. This barrier is situated between T7 and T8; it is a point of support for the spine and ribs, the back, the hypochondrium and the diaphragm. Control of this barrier enables balanced energetic exchanges between the thorax and the belly. This barrier corresponds with VG9 *Zhi Yang*, 'reaching *Yang*', the place where *Yang* is concentrated. *Ge Shu* 17Bl, the *Shu* point of the diaphragm, is found to one side.

each other at the level of *Tan Zhong*: if the opening movement is correct, the middle fingers separate without pulling the hands. This displacement is modest to begin with, but it becomes very clear with good practice. These exercises should not involve the lumbar vertebrae or the shoulders. In order not to confuse them with the movements of thoracic breathing, and to facilitate thoracic mobility, it is best to use reverse breathing in this exercise: exhale while opening the chest, inhale while hollowing the chest, this also helps to control the abdominal breathing.

In this sequence, all the postures that require the hands to be pushed upwards are especially intended for stretching the back and chest. In the preparation, the simplest approach is not to worry too much about it, but simply to relax the shoulders. Pushing the top of the head upwards, while maintaining the pelvis in a good position, is sufficient to stretch the back naturally and decrease tension or even free it completely from tension. Mental relaxation and soft, regular abdominal breathing make this action easier. This posture can be improved further by very slightly hollowing the chest, without arching, and is particularly recommended for those with a tendency to thrust the chest out.

This absence of dorsal and thoracic tension is the key to a good posture of the trunk enabling good circulation of *Qi*.

The sky: the head

Push *Bai Hui* GV20 upwards. More often than not, just visualising this push at the top of the head is enough to cause the chin to tuck in naturally and to decrease cervical lordosis by the stretch produced. Sometimes the sensation is difficult to experience. In fact a deliberate movement can be made at the level of the third barrier – *Yu Zhen Guan*,[28] the occiput, i.e. the very mobile cranio-cervical joint. Pushing the suboccipital zone (the top of the nape of the neck)

---

28 *Yu Zhen Guan* 玉枕關: the jade pillow. *Yu*: jade. *Zhen*: pillow. This barrier is found at the level of the occiput.

forwards causes a projection of the chin, a backwards tilting of the head and a feeling of pinching in the suboccipital area. Pushing this zone backwards causes the chin to draw in, a forwards tilting of the head and a feeling of stretching in the suboccipital area, but also, which is more important, a feeling of rising at the top of the head and tension in *Bai Hui*. It is this movement that enables us to become aware of *Bai Hui* in order to gather the energy of the sky.

This pushing of *Bai Hui* is naturally accompanied by a lowering of the shoulder blades and shoulders and by a relaxation of the muscles of the scapular belt. For Professor Zhang Guangde, the key to this movement is 'to raise *Bai Hui* lower the shoulders, to lower the shoulders, push *Bai Hui*'.

THE POSTURES

As they are stretches, to be effective they require the following:

- *Concentration*: in order to establish that the stretching is taking place in the correct area. This concentration is made easier by relaxation, calm abdominal breathing, slow movements, and by the experiencing the sensations caused by the stretching.

- *Breathing*: abdominal, regular. It is very important not to obstruct the breathing. If the breathing is not regular, it will be because the movement is too extreme. It is essential to find the balance between feeling the stretching and maintaining regular, calm breathing.

- *Movement*: the stretching must be the maximum possible without being painful or obstructing the breathing. It must be located in the correct area: thoracic when the arms are pushed upwards, lumbar when the hands are pushed downwards.

1. Push the hands upward, look at the sky

In this exercise it is important not to raise the shoulders while lifting the hands and not to arch the lower back. The stretching is not expressed in the shoulders or the lower back. The tension of the stretching should be felt primarily at the thoracic level, in particular between the points of the shoulder blades (the barrier *Jia Ji Guan*). The movement begins at the pelvis (retroversion) and is then transmitted to the thorax (opening), then to the shoulders, the elbows and the hands.

While maintaining the retroversion of the pelvis, raise the hands, palms upwards, if possible as far as *Tan Zhong* CV17, keeping them in contact with the body, without raising the elbows or the shoulders. As the elbows are not raised, the belly then the chest will grow slightly hollow while following the hands. In fact, it is this movement of the body that guides the hands and not the reverse.

The key to this movement is: 'lower the elbows to raise the hands'.

Then open the chest (without arching the lower back). The forward movement of *Jia Ji Guan* causes a thoracic extension, which is experienced through the opening of the chest, the projection of the sternum and rise of *Tan Zhong*, bringing the gaze slightly upwards. The opening of the chest initiates the rotational movement of the shoulders, then the elbows, then the wrists. The palms thus turn through 360°. Then, raise the hands, pushing *Tan Zhong* and the chest upwards, bringing the elbows closer together and finally pushing the wrists. The gaze is on the hands, but the stretching is felt at the thoracic level. Then, return the head to upright, *Bai Hui* upwards, without changing the posture of the trunk, so maintaining this thoracic stretching. It is essential that this basic posture is correct in order to continue the sequence successfully.

The key to this movement is: 'push the chest upwards'.

2. Lean the body to the left then to the right

Do not think of 'folding' but of 'pushing'. In order to lean to the left push the side of the chest to the right. Naturally, the movement is thoracic rather than lumbar, the stretching of the thorax is better experienced, the balance of the body is preserved, the hands remain above the head and the gaze remains forwards. Above all do not turn the trunk or look downwards.

The key is: 'to lean on one side, push the other side'.

3. Support the sky while turning the body

Here it is necessary to master the order of the movement while maintaining the basic posture. Control the retroversion of the pelvis, then turn only the hips to the maximum: the body turns by approximately 30°. Stabilise this position by drawing in the buttocks to immobilise the pelvis, then turn the back to the maximum without arching the lower back, then turn the head. Do not lean the body in any way while turning; concentrate on the shoulder which moves backwards rather than the one that advances. The feeling of stretching and maximum rotation remains thoracic.

The key is: 'turn the hips and the pelvis, then the trunk, then the neck'.

4. Open the chest by bending backwards

It is necessary to extend the thoracic extension of the first movement. This is possible thanks to the two preceding movements. Although there is also a lumbar stretching in order for the chest to move upwards, it is not a lumbar hyper-extension. In order to further extend the arms the chest should be pushed upwards. The hands are in line with *Tan Zhong*.

The key is: 'push the chest upwards'.

5. Bend the hips, lift the coccyx

It is necessary to keep the body upright; the thorax is stretched but do not think of bending forwards. On the contrary, concentrate on the movement of the coccyx. It is the action of pushing the coccyx backwards and upwards, without hollowing the lower back, which creates the inflection of the hips. Throughout the descent it is necessary to maintain this pushing of the coccyx backwards and upwards. This enables the descent to be extensive and achieved without effort. A tension then appears in the bottom of the lower back and behind the thighs. When the inflection reaches its maximum, keep the hands and fingers parallel to the ground, even if unable to touch it. To increase the extent of the movement, draw the coccyx upwards and push the heels of the hands downwards.

The key is in the title: 'bend the hips, lift the coccyx'.

6. Lift the coccyx and turn to the left

It is not the hands that turn. The rotation begins at the hips (the pelvis turns), then only the lumbar region, the hands following while remaining aligned with the trunk.

The key is: 'turn the lower back'.

7. Lift the coccyx and turn to the right

The key is the same: 'turn the lower back'.

8. Bend the hips, lift the coccyx

The preceding lumbar rotational movements make it possible with this movement to make the inflection of the hips and lumbar vertebrae to an even greater extent than before.

The key is: 'in order to bend the hips, lift the coccyx'.

9. The white chimpanzee folds its body

This movement poses many difficulties. At least the half the people beginning *Dao Yin* are unable to lower the buttocks completely while the heels remain on the ground. However, when it can be done, this posture is comfortable. It is important to divide the movement up and, even if it is limited, to be satisfied with the experience of stretching in the lumbar region as soon as it appears, without lowering the head and the trunk in order to go down further.

There is an order to follow. Bending the knees, bring them in line with the feet, and then make a maximum retroversion of the pelvis. Then, lower the buttocks in order to sit on or near the heels. In this movement the pelvis descends and therefore the trunk gradually straightens.

When the movement is limited, it is particularly important not to lean forward. The pelvis must be lowered while drawing in the buttocks as much as possible and pushing them towards the heels, which brings the trunk upwards. It is sufficient to feel the stretching at the base of the lumbar region. Gradually with practice, the extent of the movement will increase.

The key is: 'draw in the buttocks and sit down on the heels'.

10. Stretch the legs, lift the coccyx

The key is: 'in order to straighten the legs, lift the coccyx'.

11. The dragonfly embraces the column

In order not to create cervical or dorsal tension, do not try to bring the chin closer to the knees. The stretching is felt at the base of the lower back and behind the thighs and calves.

The key is: 'place the belly and the chest in front of the thighs'.

12. Return to the standing position

While it is the head that raises the body, do not make an extension of the neck. It is necessary to keep the same position of the head in relation to the neck and the trunk throughout the return. The head is raised but the movement comes from the lower back.

The key is: 'raise the head'.

13. Open the wings to regulate the breathing

The body must be kept upright. To rise up, press on the ground with the toes, open the chest and lift *Bai Hui*. To descend, draw in the buttocks and lower them towards the heels. The inflection is limited, the knees should not exceed the point of the feet, and the heels remain on the ground.

When the arms are opened, the elbows slightly bent, lightly push the inside of the elbows forwards without moving the hands. This subtle movement is difficult to control at the beginning. It permits the correct positioning of the shoulders to facilitate deep exhalation and enables the sequence 'lower the shoulders, then the elbows, then the hands' in the movement.

The key is: 'to rise, press with the toes and lift *Bai Hui*; to descend, draw in the buttocks, advance the elbows'.

APPENDIX 6

Abdominal Breathing, Techniques for Progression

André Perret

These progressive techniques are based on the sensations experienced. Each stage corresponds to a new sensation. If an exercise causes breathlessness, relax your attention, and then let your own natural breathing settle calmly before starting again at the preceding stage.

POSTURE

All these exercises of abdominal breathing can be practised lying on the back, sitting or standing. However, reverse abdominal breathing is more difficult to control when reclining.

Standing or seated, adopt the simplest posture, relaxed but with the body upright, the feet shoulder width apart.

In the standing posture the legs can be extended at the beginning, in order to concentrate only on the breathing, but later abdominal breathing is easier to control with the knees slightly bent. A hand placed on the lower belly can monitor the movements in the abdomen. To experience the breath, or its absence, in the thorax, at the beginning it is helpful to place the other hand on the chest. Later, to observe the movement in reverse abdominal breathing, this hand should be moved onto the lumbar region.

But once control has been acquired it is best to practise the respiratory exercises using exactly the method advised by Professor Zhang Guangde in Part 2 of this volume, 'Guiding and Harmonising Energy to Regulate the Breath'. In this method, the hand placed on *Dan Tian* registers the movements of the lower belly; the hand on the waist can perceive the movements of the chest (which also raise the lower ribs, creating a stretching felt between the thumb and the index finger) and the lumbar movements (which push the thumb backwards).

CONTROLLING NATURAL BREATHING

Natural breathing in the resting state should be abdominal. Unfortunately, for some people this is not the case. The description of the progressive stages towards reversed abdominal breathing therefore begins here with the basic stage important for those who have not felt abdominal breathing before. Others, after confirming that a stage has been acquired, should pass on to the following stage.

Place the left hand on the lower belly, under the navel, on *Dan Tian*. Place the right hand on the chest between the breasts at the level of *Tan Zhong* CV17. Once in this position, naturally drop the elbows in order to experience the mental and physical relaxation that supports abdominal breathing.

Breathe naturally without forcing and feel what occurs beneath your hands. If, during inhalation, the right hand, on the chest, is raised by thoracic pressure, this indicates that your natural breathing is thoracic. If it is the left hand that rises during inhalation, this is abdominal pressure, and indicates that your breathing is abdominal.

CHANGING FROM THORACIC BREATHING TO ABDOMINAL BREATHING

In order to facilitate abdominal breathing it is necessary to remove all obstacles to the flow of air when exhaling; the best method is to place the tongue on the floor of the mouth, which is half-opened, with the lips relaxed. As there then is no obstacle, air is expelled through the mouth without noise. This expelled air is also warmer and wetter (it would mist a window pane or a mirror in front of the mouth).

Without trying to change the inhalation, it is now necessary to concentrate on the exhalation, progressively trying to prolong it. If the exhalation is thoracic, the chest grows hollow under the right hand, but at the end of the exhalation the left hand also feels the belly grow hollow. Now try, without forcing, to prolong this abdominal stage more and more deeply. At the beginning, if control is difficult, assist this abdominal exhalation with a very light pressure of the hand to push the belly back. Then inhale naturally. Gradually, you will be able to control this abdominal force earlier and earlier in the exhalation and keep it going for a longer period of time.

Control of this abdominal exhalation must be progressive, with complete physical and mental relaxation. Imagine that the exhalation is like an increasingly long sigh of relief. By prolonging your abdominal exhalation, the volume of air exhaled increases and the following thoracic inhalation will then gradually decrease without further effort. It is essential to feel the abdominal movement when concentrating on the idea of displacing air by emptying the belly and forgetting the thoracic movement.

When you manage to control the abdominal push that prolongs the exhalation, try to slow down the inhalation naturally. To do that, inhale simply through the nose, the tip of the tongue touching the palate: the action known as *Que Qiao* 'raising the magpie bridge'. Continue the exercise: inhale through the nose, exhale by the mouth, gaining more and more control of the abdominal exhalation.

GIVING UP THORACIC BREATHING

At this stage your control of the out-breath is such that you will naturally inhale without needing to use the chest. After each consciously prolonged abdominal exhalation, you should relax in order to feel that the air naturally comes in to fill the vacuum that you have created. This air pushes the belly, so it returns to its natural place. It will even inflate a little. However, if the chest rises under your hand at the end of the inhalation, you should once again make your increasingly long exhalation earlier, in order to make this thoracic inhalation gradually disappear, without becoming breathless.

NATURAL ABDOMINAL BREATHING

Always adopting the same posture, continue slow abdominal breathing, but trying to regulate the breathing, that is to say equalising the duration of the inhalation and the exhalation. Ensure using the hand that the chest does not inflate during inhalation. Progressively, the breathing becomes regular, calm, soft, effortless and natural, bringing a great deal of mental and physical relaxation. From this stage onward always inhale through the nose, but exhalation may be either by the mouth or the nose.

STRENGTHENING ABDOMINAL BREATHING

Increasingly deep breathing produces sensations at the level of *Dan Tian* and *Ming Men*.

Finding *Dan Tian*

Gradually, increase the force by prolonging the end of the abdominal exhalation more and more actively. The belly is pear shaped, like a bellows, slowly emptied with force, pushing the diaphragm back and the air upwards. Being increasingly deep, this exhalation makes it possible gradually to feel this pressure and thus become aware of the diaphragm. This awareness then makes it possible to prolong the inhalation voluntarily, without thoracic movement. The diaphragm descends and actively pushes the belly and the abdominal hand back. Balance the duration of the exhalation and inhalation. Feel the forces and the movement inside the belly, like the internal tension of a balloon as it inflates and the external pressure which deflates it. There then appears a sensation as if there is a hot ball in the lower belly, moving calmly and deeply, in rhythm with the breathing: *Dan Tian*.

Finding *Ming Men*

Keep a hand on *Dan Tian* and place the other on the lower back at the level of *Shen Shu* Bl23. The inhalation must cause an abdominal expansion and a light lumbar expansion felt under the hands. If there is no lumbar expansion this means that the position of your pelvis is not correct.

The correct position of the pelvis requires you to 'draw in the buttocks' while 'relaxing the lower back'. But it is essential to keep the body and the head upright, keep the back erect and the hips square. This is a movement of retroversion (tilting the pelvis backwards) around the hips: the feeling experienced is that the coccyx slides downwards, forwards a little, then upwards (describing a small arc). At the same time, this movement involves the stretching in the lumbar region and the retraction of the third vertebra, which is felt beneath the hand: lumbar lordosis decreases or disappears.

Some people have never experienced this movement. To become aware of it, it is first necessary to practise the opposite movement 'push the buttocks out', then gradually and gently return to the natural position, then try to continue beyond. With a little training, awareness of this movement enables it to be controlled directly. This movement is easier and fuller when the knees are slightly bent.

In *Dao Yin* the postures and movements always begin with this movement, which produces a distinct sensation in the lumbar region, in particular at the level of *Ming Men* GV4 and *Shen Shu* Bl23. This feeling of stretching, of fullness, is even stronger at the time of the inhalation.

REVERSE ABDOMINAL BREATHING

At the end of the inhalation tighten the anus and the perineum, the pressure inside the lower belly increases, and then relax to exhale. Gradually, begin the contraction of the anus earlier in the inhalation. Maintain this contraction until the end of the inhalation, regardless of the additional abdominal pressure. The following exhalation is then even easier thanks to the pressure and the energy accumulated in the lower belly. In reversed abdominal inhalation the contraction of the anus is accompanied by the contraction of the abdominal muscles that limit the abdominal expansion. You then feel more and more clearly the lumbar expansion under your hand. The diaphragm resists the abdominal pressure and pushes the lumbar zone back. Gradually, the force of the diaphragm, the pressure on the lower belly and the pressure on the lower back increases. A feeling of heat and internal force moving appears even more clearly in the lower belly: *Dan Tian*. The movement of the lungs is felt in the lower back: *Ming Men*. This respiratory force extends as far as the heels. Thus, as the Master Taoist *Zhuang Zi* said, 'With his own breath, the Wise Man controls the rooting of the heel which attaches him to the ground.'

Reversed abdominal breathing reinforces the diaphragm, increasing the range of its movements and thus the exchange of gases. It massages and stimulates the internal organs. It invigorates *Dan Tian* and *Ming Men*. It supports the energetic action linking the kidney and the lung in breathing, and reinforces the relationship between the pre-heaven and post-heaven sources; it supports *Yuan Qi* and its diffusion throughout the body.

This requires a great deal of attention and control by the beginner. Until it becomes completely natural, continue to use simple abdominal breathing in the practice of *Dao Yin Yang Sheng Gong*. In order that reversed breathing may also become natural, begin by using it in the preparation sequence specifically developed by Professor Zhang Guangde: *Dao Qi Ling He Tiao Xi Gong*, 'Guiding and Harmonising Energy to Regulate the Breath' (Part 2 in this volume).

BRIEF ANATOMY OF THE RESPIRATORY SYSTEM

The human trunk is like a large cylinder, closed at the bottom and open at the top (the respiratory tracts), in which the interior is separated by the diaphragm into two parts:

1. The thorax, where the lungs are, and which is bounded by the thoracic spine, ribs and the sternum.

2. The abdomen, bounded by the pelvis and pelvic muscles, the lumbar spine, the abdominal wall and lumbar muscles.

These two zones are extendable in diameter and therefore in volume, but are also limited, first by the action of the vertebro-costal joints and then by the elasticity of the muscles of the abdominal wall. Between the thorax and the abdomen, the movements of the diaphragm upwards (inhalation) and from top to bottom (exhalation) will also modify their volumes.

But the role of breathing is to modify substantially the volume above the diaphragm, because the goal is the pulmonary exchange of air. The diaphragm acts like a piston inside a cylinder, displacing air when it goes up and pulling in air when it goes down.

The greater the magnitude of change in volume above the diaphragm, the greater the pulmonary exchange of air. These variations of volume depend on:

- the extent of the stretching (exhalation) and contraction (inhalation) of the muscle fibres of the diaphragm

- the magnitude of the movements of widening (opening with the inhalation) and contracting (closing with the exhalation) of the rib cage

- the extent of the movements of contraction (exhalation) and stretching (inhalation) of the abdominal muscles.

These three phenomena are always linked to some extent; they are all involved at the time of great effort. On the other hand, natural breathing when at rest is primarily due to the movements of the diaphragm. Natural exhalation is passive, related to muscular relaxation and the abdominal pressure. Natural inhalation, due only to the contractions of the diaphragmatic muscles, includes first an abdominal phase of descent of the diaphragm which will push back the internal organs and make the belly inflate, and a second, thoracic phase of rising in the bottom ribs to widen the thorax.

The respiratory techniques of *Dao Yin* seek to reinforce the magnitude and power of the movements of the abdominal phase of rise and descent of the diaphragm, in order to produce a natural breathing sparing in energy and very effective for the pulmonary exchange of air: slow, long, soft, deep, regular. This breathing is therefore important for health and longevity.

The diaphragm and natural breathing

The diaphragm has the shape of a cupola surrounded by muscles that attach it to the thoracic and lumbar walls. Its striated muscles have an automatic activity, but they can also have an action that is consciously controllable. They fit into the bottom of the sternum, the bottom ribs, and behind and much lower by two muscular pillars which descend almost vertically as far as the second and third lumbar vertebrae (at the level of *Ming Men*). These two posterior pillars, attached well below the rib cage, are of great importance in understanding that it is possible, through the posture, sensations, the will and *Dao Yin* techniques, to increase the amplitude of the movements of the diaphragm.

The thorax and active inhalation

Thoracic inhalation comes from a complex movement of the ribs, which combines rising and opening in order to widen the diameter of the chest. It brings into play the intercostal muscles, which make it possible to inhale (and also to exhale) more deeply. But forced thoracic inhalation also mobilises many additional muscles, which rely for their support on the cervical vertebrae and the upper limbs. It is a useful complementary inhalation at the time of effort or respiratory insufficiency, but very exhausting and distressing, especially when caused by stress. In relaxing practice, and of course in *Dao Yin*, it is essential to give up this thoracic inhalation; this is why it is initially necessary to concentrate on the exhalation phase.

The abdomen and active exhalation

Whereas the inhalation passively stretches the abdominal muscles (*rectus abdominis*, transverse and oblique), their contraction enables an exhalation created by two actions: the ribs are drawn downward, thereby decreasing the diameter of the chest, the internal organs are pushed back, driving the diaphragm upwards. In *Dao Yin* it is this second action on the stretching of the muscles of the diaphragm that interests us, as because of it the diaphragm can rise higher and thereby increase the exhaled volume of air. This action can be isolated from the first if the contraction takes place in the lower part of the abdomen: the zone of *Dan Tian*.

When diaphragmatic and abdominal breathing is well controlled, the power of contraction of the muscles of the diaphragm to make it descend even further can also be reinforced. Reverse abdominal breathing is used to do this. The abdominal and pelvic muscles contract with the inhalation and limit the swelling of the belly, forcing the diaphragm to descend while sustaining a pressure against this greater force. The diaphragm will descend while pushing the lumbar muscles back, whose passive stretching will be felt. The technique of reverse abdominal breathing depends on correctly positioning the second and third lumbar vertebrae where the pillars of the diaphragm attach at the level of *Ming Men*.

APPENDIX 7

The International Institute of *Dao Yin Yang Sheng Gong* The School of Professor Zhang Guangde

The International Institute of *Dao Yin Yang Sheng Gong* (IIDYYSG) is a 'not for profit' association under the French law of 1901, founded in 2005 at the request of Professor Zhang Guangde, the creator of the *Dao Yin Yang Sheng Gong* system. This project was made possible by the active involvement of Doctor André Perret and Professor Zhu Mian Sheng, both specialists in Chinese traditional medicine, seventh duan of *Dao Yin Yang Sheng Gong*, founders and respectively president and vice president of this association.

OBJECTIVES

- To teach and disseminate *Dao Yin Yang Sheng Gong* in Europe.

- To encourage cultural exchanges concerning health between East and West.

- To train people in the correct knowledge of the technique and theory of the *Dao Yin Yang Sheng Gong* system.

- To train people to become capable of teaching this method.

- To encourage technical, theoretical and clinical research in this system.

ACTIVITIES

Training

In the four years from 2005 to 2009, the IIDYYSG organized training courses in Biarritz for initiation and also the training of teachers in *Dao Yin Yang Sheng Gong*. These courses were directed by Professor Zhang Guangde himself.

This extensive programme was designed by Professor Zhang Guangde to provide a global understanding and detailed knowledge of his method.

The theoretical and practical teaching programme consisted of 432 hours of training for 29 different sequences of *Dao Yin* and *Yang Sheng Tai Ji*.

More than 500 practitioners from France and ten other countries benefited from the whole or part of this exceptional teaching programme.

At the end of 2009, as envisaged, Professor Zhang Guangde relinquished his teaching post in Biarritz because of his advancing years.

Publications

In order to create future publications, all Professor Zhang Guangde's courses and conferences were filmed and archived.

Throughout the training programme at the IIDYYSG, Professor Zhang Guangde, Zhu Mian Sheng and André Perret met regularly in order to discuss theoretical and practical issues of teaching and practice, and also to consider the fields of clinical and theoretical research appropriate to each sequence and to the method in general.

In 2010, the training programme came to an end, and the IIDYYSG devoted itself purely to the publication of the translations in French, then in English, of the books of Professor Zhang Guangde.

Each book includes:

- The technical and theoretical explanation of each sequence in its entirety, written by Professor Zhang Guangde.

- Appendices and comments written by Zhu Mian Sheng and André Perret.

- A demonstration DVD.

The translation from Chinese to French is by Zhu Mian Sheng, and the translation from French to English is by Mark Atkinson.

Research

In order to continue clinical, technical and theoretical research into *Dao Yin*, a research group has been formed, comprising Zhu Mian Sheng and André Perret and several graduates of the IIDYYSG, alumni of Professor Zhang Guangde.

Zhu Mian Sheng

Born in 1948 in Kunming, Yunnan.

Graduate of Chinese Traditional Medicine of Yunnan and Beijing.

Professor of the University of Medicine and Chinese Traditional Pharmacopeia of Beijing.

Associate Professor of the Institute of Chinese Traditional Medicine of Yunnan and the Institute of Western Medicine of Kunming.

Senior consultant in TCM.

Graduate of Medical Anthropology at the Faculty of Medicine, University of Paris 13.

Doctor of Social Sciences (option Health), University of Paris 13.

External expert of the AFSSAPS for the Chinese pharmacopoeia.

Practitioner of Chinese traditional medicine since 1976.

Resident in France since 1987.

Teacher of Chinese traditional medicine with the Faculty of Medicine, University Paris 13, since 1989.

Director of the diploma of Chinese Traditional Medicine in this faculty since 1997.

Member of the office of the World Federation of Medicine and Chinese Traditional Pharmacopoeia (WFCMS) in Beijing since 2004.

President of the Pan-European federation of the specialists in Chinese traditional medicine (PEFCTCM) since 2002.

Author of numerous books published in China.

Published in France:

- *Breathing and Energy* (medical *Qi Gong*).

- *Know How to Eat to Know How to Live* (Chinese dietetic).

- *Time, Points, Space* (chrono acupuncture).

Author of more than 70 articles in China and elsewhere, in international congresses and international reviews of TCM.

Director of the editorial board of the *International Sino-French Prescriptive Nomenclature of Words and Basic Expressions of Chinese Medicine* under the direction of the WFCMS (in progress).

Cofounder, and vice president of the International Institute of DYYSG in Biarritz since 2005.

André Perret

B orn in 1955 in Bayonne.

Doctorate in Medicine in 1984.

Diploma of Acupuncture from the French School of Acupuncture.

University Degree of Chinese Traditional Medicine.

University Degree of Homeopathy.

University Degree of Osteopathy.

University Degree of Sports Medicine.

Emeritus Professor of the University of Chinese Medicine of Yunnan.

Practising *Dao Yin Yang Sheng Gong* since 1988 with teachers of the University of Chinese Medicine of Kunming, and since 1995 with the teachers of the Beijing Sports University, in particular Professor Zhang Guangde.

Participated in the international tournaments of *Dao Yin* in Beijing in 1995 and in Hangzhou in 1997.

Awarded seventh duan *Dao Yin Yang Sheng Gong* in 2007 (Beijing Sports University).

Teacher of *Dao Yin Yang Sheng Gong* within Association Kunming from 1992 to 2009.

Teacher of *Dao Yin Yang Sheng Gong* for several years with the faculty of Northern Paris UFR health, within the framework of the University Diploma of Chinese Traditional Medicine.

Since 1998 presented two university dissertations on the use of *Dao Yin* in chronic dorso-lumbagos: a clinical study and an orthopaedic study.

Presented his work to the International Congress of Chinese Medicine, the congress of General medicine of Medec and in other Symposiums.

Cofounder of Kunming Association in 1989.

Cofounder and president of the IIDYYSG since 2005.

Mark Atkinson

Born in 1946 in Yorkshire.

Bachelor of Education Degree from Birmingham University in 1969.

Thirty-year career as schoolteacher, including 15 years as Head Teacher in Jersey (Channel Islands).

Practising *Taiji Quan* since 1980, and *Dao Yin Yang Sheng Gong* since 1993 when he met and worked with Professor Zhang Guangde in China as his first English student.

Introduced Professor Zhang and his work into the UK in 1994.

Subsequently worked with Professor Zhang and other teachers from the Beijing Sports University, in China, the US, France, Portugal and Germany.

Participated in the international tournament of *Dao Yin* in Beijing in 1995 and at that time was also granted Senior Judge status of the China Dao Yin Association.

Created '*Ru Zhi Di Zi*' (outstanding and close disciple) of Professor Zhang and his English representative in May 1999.

Awarded 6th duan *Dao Yin Yang Sheng Gong* in 2006 (Beijing Sports University).

Founder and first President of the English *Dao Yin Yang Sheng Gong* Association 1999, authorised by Professor Zhang to accredit teachers of DYYSG in the UK.

Founder and Principal Teacher of the Dao Yin Taiji Centre in Jersey (Channel Islands) 1990–2000.

Founder and current Principal Teacher of L'Association *Chung Fu* in the Charente Maritime in France, where he now lives.

Member of the Conseil d'Administration of the IIDYYSG since 2005.